GLACIERS

EARLY BIRD
EARTH SCIENCE

BY SALLY M. WALKER

LERNER PUBLICATIONS COMPANY • MINNEAPOLIS

Lerner Publications Company
A division of Lerner Publishing Group, Inc.
241 First Avenue North
Minneapolis, MN 55401 U.S.A.

Website address: www.lernerbooks.com

Library of Congress Cataloging-in-Publication Data

Walker, Sally M.
    Glaciers / by Sally M. Walker.
       p.   cm. — (Early bird earth science)
    Includes index.
    ISBN 978–0–8225–6737–0 (lib. bdg. : alk. paper)
    1. Glaciers—Juvenile literature. I. Title.
GB2403.8W34 2008
551.31'2—dc22   2006036727

Manufactured in the United States of America
1 2 3 4 5 6 – JR – 13 12 11 10 09 08

CONTENTS

4

BE A WORD DETECTIVE

Can you find these words as you read about glaciers? Be a detective and try to figure out what they mean. You can turn to the glossary on page 46 for help.

cirque	firn	ice shelf
crevasse	global warming	moraine
erratic	icebergs	valley glacier
evaporate	ice sheet	

Huge piles of snow and ice are common in cold places. What do you call a huge, icy pile that starts to move?

CHAPTER 1
WHAT IS A GLACIER?

Have you ever seen a pile of snow? Very cold places have many piles of snow. In these places, snow never completely melts. Every time it snows, the piles get bigger. They can grow big enough to cover mountains! The piles get very icy too. Sometimes a huge, icy pile starts to move. Then it is called a glacier.

6

Many glaciers are enormous. They can be more than 60 miles long. It would take a car driving on a highway about one hour to travel that distance.

Glaciers can also be very tall. A glacier can be more than 15,000 feet tall. That's about nine times as tall as the world's tallest building.

Some glaciers grow to be gigantic. Their icy peaks reach high into the sky.

Some glaciers look like blankets. Others look like rivers made of ice. But glaciers don't move as fast as rivers. Some glaciers move just a few yards every year. A fast glacier might move 1,000 feet in one year. One speedy glacier in Greenland moves about 113 feet per day.

Jakobshavn, Greenland, is home to the world's fastest-moving glacier.

Glaciers and snowy mountains line Antarctica's Lemaire Channel.

Glaciers form in places where it stays cold all year. Antarctica is one of these places. Antarctica is cold even in the summertime. Many glaciers form in Antarctica. Much of Greenland stays cold all year too. Greenland is another place where many glaciers form.

Glaciers also form on the tops of tall mountains. There is a glacier on Mount Kilimanjaro in Africa.

Glaciers are made up of millions of tiny snowflakes.

Every glacier on Earth formed from snowflakes. But how do snowflakes turn into glaciers?

CHAPTER 2
HOW DO GLACIERS FORM?

If you look closely at a snowflake, you can see sharp, icy points. A snowflake's first step to becoming a glacier starts when some of those points evaporate. *Evaporate* means "change from a solid material to a gas."

Heat from the sun causes some of the points to evaporate. When sun shines down on the icy points, they change into a gas called water vapor. The water vapor seeps into tiny air spaces in a snowflake.

Snowflakes are mostly made of air spaces. Do you see air spaces in these snowflakes?

A snowflake begins to turn into glacial ice when water freezes in the center of the flake.

The snowflake is starting to become glacial ice. Cold air chills the water vapor. When the water vapor gets cold, it changes into water. The water trickles to the center of a snowflake. In the snowflake's center, the water freezes into ice.

The water also freezes around some of the snowflake's pointy edges. The snowflake doesn't look sharp and pointy anymore. It starts to become round. After about two months, the snowflake looks a little like a ball of ice.

Snowflakes take on a rounded shape when water freezes around their edges.

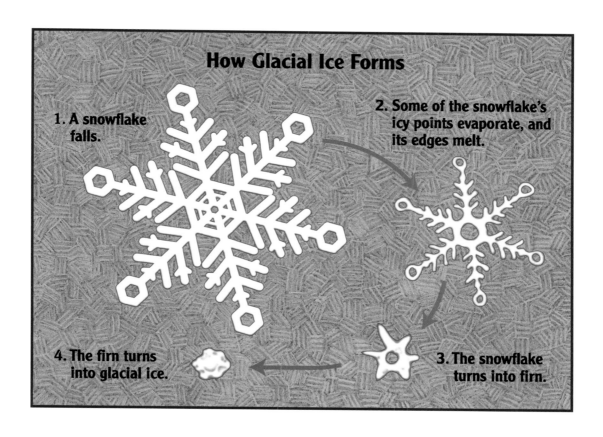

How Glacial Ice Forms

1. A snowflake falls.

2. Some of the snowflake's icy points evaporate, and its edges melt.

4. The firn turns into glacial ice.

3. The snowflake turns into firn.

Rounded snowflakes that last through a summer are called firn. Over time, new snow falls on top of the firn. The weight of the new snow squeezes the firn together. It squeezes out the air that is in between the pieces of firn. When almost all of the air is squeezed out, the firn becomes glacial ice.

You can't make glacial ice by freezing water in your freezer. Glacial ice is made from old snowflakes that have melted slightly, been squeezed, and then frozen again.

In places where a lot of snow falls, glacial ice may form in about 20 years. In places where little snow falls, it may take more than 100 years for glacial ice to form.

It takes many years for snowflakes to turn into glacial ice.

This is a valley glacier. It is one of two main types of glaciers. What is the other type of glacier called?

CHAPTER 3

DIFFERENT KINDS OF GLACIERS

There are two main types of glaciers. One type is called a valley glacier. The other type is called an ice sheet.

A valley glacier begins to form inside a cirque (sehrk). A cirque is a bowl-shaped hollow near the top of a mountain. Snow falls into the cirque. The air on a mountaintop is very cold. So the snow doesn't melt.

Mountain cirques are easy to spot. They look like holes left behind by giant ice-cream scoops.

Snow collects in cirques. The snow builds up until it is very deep.

Each time it snows, the snow inside the cirque gets deeper. Over time, the snow turns into firn. Eventually, the firn turns into glacial ice. The cirque gets filled completely. There is not enough room for the glacial ice to fit inside the cirque.

The glacier flows out of the cirque. It moves down the side of the mountain. It spreads downward into the mountain's valley. A valley is a low place between mountains. When the glacier spreads into a valley, it becomes a valley glacier.

Valley glaciers wind their way between steep mountains.

An enorcomous ice sheet sits on Greenland. The sheet is big enough to cover the states of California, Oregon, Washington, and Idaho!

Ice sheets are larger than valley glaciers. They can be almost as large as a whole continent.

Ice sheets are very deep. They are so deep that they cover high mountains. Only the tallest mountain peaks stick out above ice sheets.

Ice sheets can cover land and even seas. Ice sheets are so big that a single ice sheet can cover both land and water. Scientists have a special name for the part of an ice sheet that covers water. The name is ice shelf.

Thick ice shelves stretch across Greenland's seas.

Sometimes chunks of ice break off of ice shelves. These chunks of ice are called icebergs. Icebergs float off into the sea.

Sometimes icebergs float near ships. Icebergs can be dangerous when they float near ships. They can crash into ships.

Icebergs drift through the water near Cierva Cove, Antarctica.

CHAPTER 4
MOVING ICE

Ocean waters push icebergs from place to place. It is easy to see how they move. But why do glaciers move on land?

Even very large glaciers skim easily over the land.

Each year, new layers of snow are added to a glacier. They press on the ice below. The pressure makes the lower layers of ice move.

Have you ever flattened a ball of clay with your hand? The pressure of your hand squeezes the clay. The clay moves and spreads away from your hand. Like clay, glacial ice moves without breaking. It bends and slides across even rough surfaces.

Scientists have a name for the way glacial ice moves. They call it plastic flow. Plastic flow lets a glacier flow out of a cirque. It makes the glacier spread across the land. Plastic flow keeps large ice sheets moving.

Plastic flow allows large mounds of ice and snow to move.

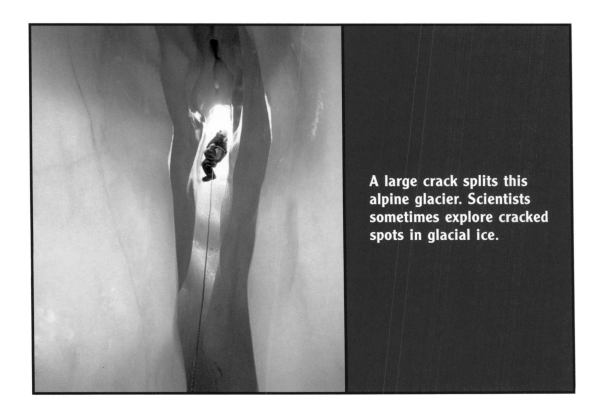

A large crack splits this alpine glacier. Scientists sometimes explore cracked spots in glacial ice.

Ice near the surface of a glacier doesn't bend. It is brittle. That means it breaks easily. A glacier often flows over bumps on the land. Deep inside the glacier, the ice bends. But brittle ice near the surface breaks.

When surface ice breaks, it sometimes leaves a crack. If the crack is very deep, it is called a crevasse (krih-VAHS).

Valley glaciers can move in another way. The whole glacier can slide.

Sometimes the ice on the bottom of a valley glacier melts a little. The melted ice makes a thin layer of water. The water helps the glacier slide. How does water help a glacier slide?

Water can make the bottom of a valley glacier slippery.

Valley glaciers slip through mountain valleys in the same way you might glide down a slippery slide in a swimming pool.

Water helps a glacier slide because it eases friction. Friction is a force that stops objects from moving. When water is between glacial ice and the ground, there is less friction. This means that the glacier can move easily.

Glaciers move at different speeds. Ice sheets move slowly. Valley glaciers move faster. No matter how fast glaciers move, one thing is certain. Glaciers change the way the land looks.

Friction prevents large ice sheets from moving quickly.

A glacier changed this landscape in Alaska's Tongass National Forest. How do glaciers change the land?

CHAPTER 5

GLACIERS AND EARTH'S SURFACE

Glaciers are very powerful. They change the land when they move. In the past, ancient glaciers shaped Earth's surface. And glaciers still shape Earth today.

When glaciers flow across land, the ice scrapes over rocks. Sometimes the ice flows into a cracked rock. The ice chips off part of the cracked rock. Cirques are made when ice chips away rock from a mountain.

Glaciers shape the rocky surfaces of mountains.

Glaciers can scoop soil away from flat areas. Big holes are left behind. The holes are called basins. Some basins fill with water. They become lakes. The Great Lakes of Canada and the northern United States are in basins that were scooped by ancient glaciers.

Lake Superior fills a deep basin carved by glaciers long ago.

Glaciers flow inside river valleys. A river valley is shaped like the letter *V*. A glacier chips away the steep valley walls. It makes the valley's shape look like the letter *U*.

Glaciers can also move gigantic boulders. A boulder carried by a glacier is called an erratic (ih-RAHT-ihk). Glaciers carry erratics far away from the places where they were made.

This erratic sits in Maine's Acadia National Park.

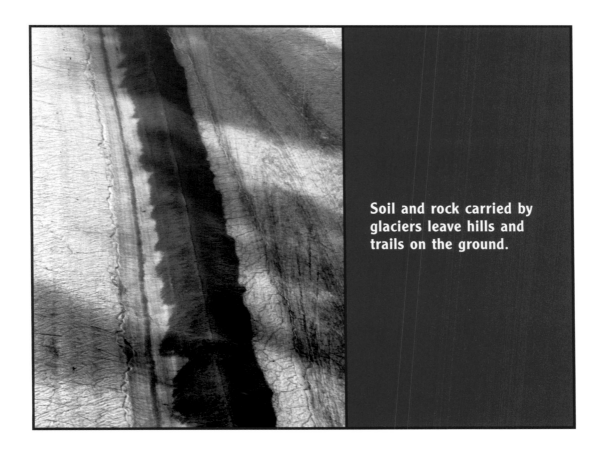

Soil and rock carried by glaciers leave hills and trails on the ground.

Glaciers scrape pieces of soil and rock from the ground. They carry the pieces with them when they move.

Glaciers melt when the air temperature warms. The pieces of soil and rock fall to the ground again. They make a hill called a moraine (moh-RAIHN).

Glaciers change Earth's surface in many ways. Glaciers form where the air is cold. If the air around glaciers gets too warm, the glaciers will melt.

For the past 100 years, Earth's air has been getting warmer. Scientists call this global warming. A gas called carbon dioxide helps cause global warming.

Have you ever left an ice cube outside on a hot day? Like an ice cube, glaciers melt when temperatures get warm.

High temperatures in the summer of 2003 caused glacial melting in Europe.

When extra carbon dioxide gets into the air, it traps heat near Earth. The sun's rays shine on Earth. They warm the soil and the air. Some of the sun's rays bounce off Earth. They head toward space. But carbon dioxide in the atmosphere traps some of the sun's rays. It stops them from going back into space. When this happens, Earth gets hotter.

Certain things people do cause Earth to get hotter. Burning fossil fuels puts carbon dioxide in the air. Gasoline and coal are types of fossil fuels. They help cars run. They help heat our homes in the winter. But they also make carbon dioxide. It gets into the air and traps the sun's heat. It helps cause global warming.

Burning coal helps make electricity. But it also speeds global warming.

People cut down forests to make room for buildings.

Fossil fuels aren't the only reason Earth is getting hotter. People sometimes cut down forests. Trees in the forest use carbon dioxide from the air. Carbon dioxide helps the trees grow. When people cut down forests, the trees are gone. They aren't there to use carbon dioxide. It stays in the air.

When carbon dioxide builds up in the air, Earth can become too warm for glaciers. The glaciers begin to melt.

Many glaciers are melting today. The glaciers on Africa's Mount Kilimanjaro are much smaller than they were 20 years ago. In Alaska, the end of Muir Glacier has melted so much that it has made a lake.

This is what Muir Glacier looked like in 1976.

This is what Muir Glacier looked like in 2003. Much of the snow and ice have melted.

What would happen if all Earth's glaciers melted? The ocean level would get higher. Many scientists believe the ocean would rise about 28 inches. The water would rise very slowly. But it might rise enough to flood some cities along the coasts.

Many people are talking about Earth's rising temperatures. They are trying to find out what we can do to protect glaciers.

Glaciers are beautiful, but they are in danger.

We can help protect glaciers by learning more about them.

Glaciers have changed Earth's surface many times. They are changing Earth's surface now. The more we study glaciers, the more we will learn about them. And they may help us understand how glaciers will change Earth in the future.

ON SHARING A BOOK

When you share a book with a child, you show that reading is important. To get the most out of the experience, read in a comfortable, quiet place. Turn off the television and limit other distractions, such as telephone calls. Be prepared to start slowly. Take turns reading parts of this book. Stop occasionally and discuss what you're reading. Talk about the photographs. If the child begins to lose interest, stop reading. When you pick up the book again, revisit the parts you have already read.

BE A VOCABULARY DETECTIVE

The word list on page 5 contains words that are important in understanding the topic of this book. Be word detectives and search for the words as you read the book together. Talk about what the words mean and how they are used in the sentence. Do any of these words have more than one meaning? You will find the words defined in a glossary on page 46.

WHAT ABOUT QUESTIONS?

Use questions to make sure the child understands the information in this book. Here are some suggestions:

What did this paragraph tell us? What does this picture show? What do you think we'll learn about next? How big is a glacier? Where do glaciers form? What are the two main types of glaciers? What is an ice shelf? What is your favorite part of this book? Why?

If the child has questions, don't hesitate to respond with questions of your own, such as What do *you* think? Why? What is it that you don't know? If the child can't remember certain facts, turn to the index.

INTRODUCING THE INDEX

The index helps readers find information without searching through the whole book. Turn to the index on page 48. Choose an entry such as *icebergs*, and ask the child to find out why icebergs can be dangerous. Repeat with as many entries as you like. Ask the child to point out the differences between an index and a glossary. (The index helps readers find information, while the glossary tells readers what words mean.)

LEARN MORE ABOUT
GLACIERS

BOOKS

Brimner, Larry Dane. *Glaciers*. New York: Children's Press, 2000. Read more about how glaciers develop and how they affect Earth.

Johnston, Joyce. *Alaska*. Minneapolis: Lerner Publications Company, 2002. This book takes you to Alaska, a state that is home to about 100,000 glaciers.

Simon, Seymour. *Icebergs and Glaciers*. New York: Morrow, 1987. Beautiful pictures bring glaciers and icebergs to life.

Storad, Conrad J. *Fossil Fuels*. Minneapolis: Lerner Publications Company, 2008. Find out all about fossil fuels in this interesting book.

WEBSITES

Climate Change Kids Site
http://epa.gov/climatechange/kids
Learn about climate change, an event that greatly affects glaciers.

Glaciers
http://library.thinkquest.org/3876/glaciers.html
This page includes diagrams and information on glaciers.

Science News for Kids
http://www.sciencenewsforkids.org
This site is packed with information on science topics. It has articles on the weather, Earth, our environment, and more.

GLOSSARY

cirque (sehrk): a bowl-shaped hollow near the top of a mountain

crevasse (krih-VAHS): a deep crack in a glacier. A crevasse is caused when the ice on a glacier's surface breaks.

erratic (ih-RAHT-ihk): a boulder carried by a glacier

evaporate (ih-VAH-poh-rate): to change from a solid material to a gas

firn: rounded snowflakes that last through a summer

global warming: the slow rise in Earth's temperature

icebergs: chunks of ice that break off of ice shelves

ice sheet: a type of glacier. Ice sheets are very large.

ice shelf: a part of an ice sheet that covers water

moraine (moh-RAIHN): a hill formed when pieces of soil and rock fall out of a melting glacier

valley glacier: a type of glacier. Valley glaciers form in hollows near the tops of mountains.

INDEX

Pages listed in **bold** type refer to photographs.